Blool Cave

Written by Jon Mayhew

Illustrated by Giorgio Bacchin

Collins

Chapter 1

Odysseus stood on the deck of his ship and gazed out across the sea at the dark island on the horizon. He and his crew had sailed for many days and they needed to find land and fresh supplies.

"That is the island of the Cyclops," said his friend Antiphon. "The men who live there are giant, one-eyed monsters."

"I bet they'll give us food," Odysseus grinned. "Especially for this." He held up a goat skin full of liquid. "This sweet water and honey from our homeland would make any man feel full and content."

Soon they reached the island of the Cyclops. Odysseus and twelve men climbed ashore, leaving the rest of the crew to watch the ship. They saw a huge cave mouth in the cliff's face. Odysseus and his men crept towards it and peered in.

"This cave is massive," Antiphon gasped.

"And full of good things to eat!" another of the men said, pushing past and running in. They followed him carefully.

All around the cave stood towering blocks of cheese and colossal buckets of sheep's milk.

"I don't like it," Antiphon said, glancing over his shoulder.

At that moment, the cave darkened. A hideous, warty-skinned giant with wiry hair and one eye in the middle of his head stood in the doorway. Thick yellow teeth poked out of his mouth. Ragged animal skins covered his strong body.

"A Cyclops!" Odysseus whispered. His men scrambled behind buckets and slabs of cheese.

A flock of huge sheep came clattering in, bleating and pushing against each other.

"Such big sheep," Odysseus whispered. "No wonder there's so much milk in the cave."

"That's it, my lovelies," the Cyclops said to the sheep in a booming voice. "Settle down. Soon it will be dark." The giant grabbed the edge of a massive circular stone and rolled it across the door. They were trapped!

The Cyclops scooped up a barrel full of milk and gulped it down. Milk trickled down his greasy beard. Suddenly, he stopped and stared over at where Odysseus was hiding.

"Who's there?" the Cyclops growled. "Come out where I can see you!" Odysseus and his men stepped out.

"And where did you come from?" the Cyclops boomed, raising his single eyebrow.

"Forgive us," Odysseus said, giving a bow. "Our ship was wrecked nearby and we smelt the beautiful cheese in your cave."
He didn't like the look of the giant and didn't want him to know about his ship.

"You stole my food!" the Cyclops roared and, without warning, snatched up two of Odysseus's men in his huge hands and greedily ate them.

Odysseus and his men looked on in horror. Some drew their swords but Odysseus stopped them.

"If we kill him now," he whispered, "then we'll never get out of the cave. We need him to roll the stone from the door."

"You're trapped," the Cyclops laughed. He stamped over to the fire in the middle of the cave and lay down beside it. "I'm going to sleep now. See you in the morning, for breakfast!" Soon, his snores shook the walls of the cave.

Chapter 2

Odysseus and his men didn't sleep that night. All they could do was wait, listen to the giant's snoring, and think about their poor friends.

Finally, morning came. The Cyclops stood and gave a huge rumbling yawn. "Ah! You're still here," he laughed. "Good, I'm starving!" He reached down and snatched up two more of Odysseus's men.

"I'll have revenge," Odysseus muttered under his breath.

The Cyclops rolled the stone from the door and let his sheep out. Odysseus and his men ran for the exit but the giant was too fast for them.

"Oh no," he laughed, swatting them away with his great hand. "I think you should stay for dinner." With an evil laugh, the Cyclops left the cave and closed the heavy stone door behind him.

"What will we do?" Antiphon sighed. "We're doomed!"

"I have a plan!" Odysseus said. He ran over to a wooden club that lay in the corner of the cave. "Help me with this!"

All day, the men hacked and sharpened the end of the club to a point.

Evening came and the rock rolled back once more. In came the Cyclops and his herd of sheep. Then the door crunched shut again.

"So you decided to stay!" he sniggered, scooping up another two men, including Antiphon. "Good! I'm starving!"

"No!" screamed Odysseus, but the Cyclops ate Odysseus's friend in one greedy gulp. Sadness and anger swept over Odysseus but he calmly crept towards the Cyclops with the goat skin full of water and honey on his shoulder.

"Great Cyclops," he said. "Now I see how powerful you are, perhaps if I give you this sweet drink, you may spare me."

"Sweet drink?" the Cyclops grunted, picking his teeth. "Let me see." He snatched the goat skin from Odysseus's hands and squeezed it over his gaping mouth until it burst. The Cyclops smacked his lips. "That's good."

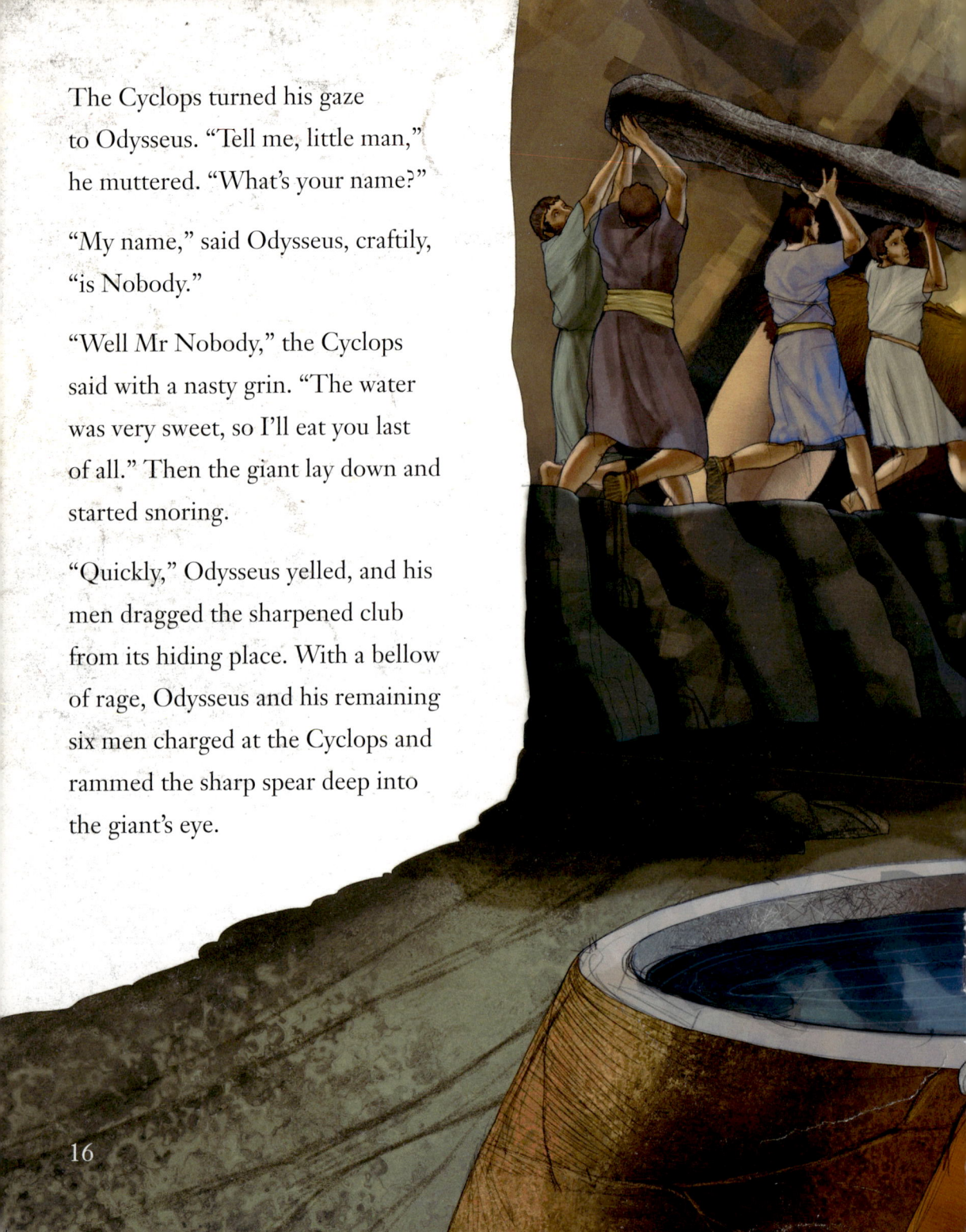

The Cyclops turned his gaze to Odysseus. "Tell me, little man," he muttered. "What's your name?"

"My name," said Odysseus, craftily, "is Nobody."

"Well Mr Nobody," the Cyclops said with a nasty grin. "The water was very sweet, so I'll eat you last of all." Then the giant lay down and started snoring.

"Quickly," Odysseus yelled, and his men dragged the sharpened club from its hiding place. With a bellow of rage, Odysseus and his remaining six men charged at the Cyclops and rammed the sharp spear deep into the giant's eye.

The Cyclops screamed in agony and staggered to his feet, pulling at the stake in his eye.

"Help, my brothers!" he called through the sealed door. "I am being murdered!"

Odysseus and his men heard the earth shake as the Cyclops's family came charging to the cave. A voice boomed through the door.

"What is all the fuss, little brother?" it called. "Who is killing you?"

"Nobody!" the Cyclops cried. "Nobody is killing me!"

"Nobody?" snorted another voice. "You woke us up to play tricks on us?"

"But Nobody is trying to kill me!" the Cyclops wept.

"Stop wasting our time!" shouted his brothers and stamped away. "Go back to bed!"

"You won't get away with this," the Cyclops hissed, fumbling around blindly for the men.

19

All the rest of the night, Odysseus and his men crept this way and that, dodging the searching fingers of the blind giant.

Once, the huge hands swept centimetres from Odysseus's head. He froze, holding his breath as the Cyclops grabbed hold of a sheep. It gave a startled bleat and he dropped it.

Odysseus had an idea. Sneaking around the cave, he tied the sheep together in threes.

At dawn, he whispered to his men to hold on to the stomachs of the sheep. One by one, his soldiers climbed under the sheep, gripping their woolly fleeces to hold on. Finally, Odysseus caught the big-horned ram that led the flock, climbed under its belly and held on tight.

Chapter 3

Morning came and the sheep began to bleat. They wanted to go out. Grumbling, the blind Cyclops rolled the stone back and then sat in the entrance.

"You won't get past me," he said, blocking the only way out.

In threes, the sheep began to walk past him. He stopped each group and ran his hands across their backs, running his warty fingers through their fleeces to make sure they were sheep and not men trying to crawl out.

Odysseus watched his men clinging to the sheep, dropping off when they were safely away and sprinting to the beach. When every sheep was out of the cave, he kicked the ram and it began to walk towards the Cyclops. The giant grabbed the ram, tangling his fingers in its fleece.

"What's this?" the Cyclops said. "Why didn't you go out first as you always do?"

Odysseus held his breath and clung to the ram as the Cyclops ran his greasy fingers all over the animal. Odysseus could see the cracked fingernails catch in the thick wool.

Finally, the ram went free and Odysseus heaved a sigh of relief. But he and his friends weren't safe yet!

"Quickly!" Odysseus called. He let go of the ram and ran to the ship with his men. Behind them they heard a furious roar. The Cyclops had realised they had escaped.

The crew who had been left with the ship lifted the sails as Odysseus climbed aboard.

"Where are you?" the Cyclops yelled, hurling a huge rock blindly in the direction of the ship. Water rained down on Odysseus and his men, and the ship rocked on the massive wave. The wind caught the sail and the men pulled at the oars, sending the ship speeding through the sea.

Odysseus looked back, thinking of his lost friends as the land of the Cyclops vanished behind him. He was glad to have escaped but he wished he'd never set foot on that island.

The Cyclops's strength

They were trapped!

The Cyclops snatched up two of Odysseus's men in his huge hands and greedily ate them.

"I think you should stay for dinner."

30

Odysseus's trickery

"Perhaps if I give you this sweet drink you may spare me."

"Nobody is killing me!"

The ram went free and Odysseus heaved a sigh of relief.

Ideas for reading

Written by Gillian Howell
Primary Literacy Consultant

Learning objectives: *(word reading objectives correspond with White band; all other objectives correspond with Sapphire band)* continue to apply phonic knowledge and skills as the route to decode words until automatic decoding has become embedded and reading is fluent; increasing their familiarity with a wide range of books, including myths, legends and traditional stories; drawing inferences such as inferring characters' feelings, thoughts and motives from their actions and justifying inferences with evidence

Curriculum links: History

Interest words: horizon, hideous, circular, revenge, stomachs, furious

Word count: 1,497

Resources: paper, pens, collage materials, whiteboard

Getting started

- Read the title together and look at the illustration. Check the children can see that the giant has one eye in the middle of his forehead. Ask if anyone has heard of a story with a character like this.

- Turn to the back cover and read the blurb together. Ask the children if they know who Odysseus is and explain that he is not a character in Ancient Greek myths. Ensure they understand what a myth is.

- Discuss the title of the story with the children. Ask them to say why they think it is called *Blood Cave*. What do they think might happen inside the cave?

- Turn to p2 and ask the children to find the words *Odysseus*, *Antiphon* and *Cyclops*. Help them to pronounce these words.

Reading and responding

- Read pp2–3 together and ask children to predict what might happen if Odysseus lands on the island. Do they think the one-eyed monsters will give them any supplies?

- Remind the children to use their knowledge of phonics and familiar spelling patterns to help them work out new words.